Happy Holidays!

Easter

by Rebecca Sabelko

BELLWETHER MEDIA
MINNEAPOLIS, MN

BLASTOFF!
Beginners

Blastoff! Beginners are developed by literacy experts and educators to meet the needs of early readers. These engaging informational texts support young children as they begin reading about their world. Through simple language and high frequency words paired with crisp, colorful photos, Blastoff! Beginners launch young readers into the universe of independent reading.

Blastoff! Universe

BLASTOFF! Beginners — Reading Level — Grade K

BLASTOFF! READERS — Grades 1-3

BLASTOFF! DISCOVERY — Grade 4

Sight Words in This Book 🔍

a	from	is	other	up
an	go	it	the	
big	have	many	they	
eat	he	of	time	
for	in	on	to	

This edition first published in 2023 by Bellwether Media, Inc.

No part of this publication may be reproduced in whole or in part without written permission of the publisher. For information regarding permission, write to Bellwether Media, Inc., Attention: Permissions Department, 6012 Blue Circle Drive, Minnetonka, MN 55343.

Library of Congress Cataloging-in-Publication Data

LC record for Easter available at: https://lccn.loc.gov/2022009288

Text copyright © 2023 by Bellwether Media, Inc. BLASTOFF! BEGINNERS and associated logos are trademarks and/or registered trademarks of Bellwether Media, Inc.

Editor: Christina Leaf   Designer: Laura Sowers

Printed in the United States of America, North Mankato, MN.

Table of Contents

It Is Easter!

It is time for
an egg hunt!
Happy Easter!

egg

What Is Easter?

Easter is in
March, April,
or May.
It is on a Sunday.

Christians honor **Jesus Christ.** They believe he rose from the dead.

Others enjoy the start of spring.

Family, Candy, and Fun!

Families go
to church.
They dress up.

13

Families eat
a big meal.
Many have lamb
or ham.

ham

Kids **dye** eggs.
They go on
egg hunts.

dyed eggs

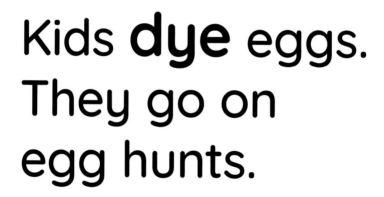

The Easter Bunny
visits. It gives
baskets
of candy.

basket

Easter is a time of joy!

Easter Facts

Celebrating Easter

dyed eggs

candy

basket

Easter Activities

go to
church

share a
meal

dye eggs

Glossary

baskets

things that are made to hold smaller objects

Christians

believers in the words of Jesus Christ

dye

to add color to something

Jesus Christ

a teacher who Christians believe is the Son of God

To Learn More

ON THE WEB

FACTSURFER

Factsurfer.com gives you a safe, fun way to find more information.

1. Go to www.factsurfer.com.

2. Enter "Easter" into the search box and click 🔍.

3. Select your book cover to see a list of related content.

Index

The images in this book are reproduced through the courtesy of: JeniFoto, front cover, p. 22; Evgeny Atamanenko, p. 3; Ekaterina Pokrovsky, pp. 4-5; Monkey Business Images, pp. 6-7, 18-19; jorisvo, pp. 8-9; jarenwickland, pp. 10-11; FatCamera, pp. 12-13; Elena Veselova, p. 14; Gpointstudio/ Image Source/ SuperStock, pp. 14-15; New Africa, p. 16; dszc, pp. 16-17; Tsekhmister, p. 18; FamVeld, pp. 20-21; jgroup, p. 22 (go to church); SeventyFour, p. 22 (share a meal); LightField Studios, p. 22 (dye eggs); TravnikovStudio, p. 23 (baskets); pixelheadphoto digitalskillet, p. 23 (Christians); Arina P Habich, p. 23 (dye); Keith McIntyre, p. 23 (Jesus Christ).

24